THE DRUNKEN TOMATO SEATTLE

A Definitive Guide to the
Best Bloody Marys in Seattle

Cheers!
Shelley Buchanan

Shelley Buchanan

Cover art design by The Drunken Tomato. Seattle skyline photo credit: Vecteezy.com/members/nightwolfdezines. Author photo credit: © 2014 Loriant

Published in the United States by

The Drunken Tomato
www.drunkentomato.com

ISBN: 978-0-9912392-4-5 (paperback)
ISBN: 978-0-9912392-3-8 (e-book)

Printed in the United States

First Edition

To vodka,
For everywhere you've been
And everywhere you're going

TABLE OF CONTENTS

NORTH

BALLARD

CENTRAL

CAPITOL HILL

DOWNTOWN

WEST SEATTLE & SOUTH

INTRODUCTION

A FTER DRINKING OVER *100* of the best and worst bloody marys that Seattle has to offer, I've learned three things. First, Seattle snubs celery, second, infused vodka reignes supreme, and third, with the exception of a very few places, Seattle bloody marys are damn expensive.

But bloody mary woes aside, I've observed creativity, innovation, and an exhilarating inspiration from the surrounding Puget Sound. From locally grown herbs and spices to locally produced pepper vodka and freshly shucked Washington oysters, Seattle bloody marys epitomize Northwest cuisine and culture.

You, no doubt, want to know who serves up the absolute best bloody mary in Seattle. But the answer lies buried within a long list of variables, including what neighborhood you're in, your mood, the weather, and of course, how hungover you are. But I know you want what you want. So here is my top 10 list, right now, subject to drunken fluctuations and in no particular order. Now go forth, and drink bloody marys.

The Drunken Tomato's
10 Best Bloody Marys in Seattle

1. Percy's

2. Fresh Bistro

3. Sam's Tavern

4. Bell + Whete

5. Capitol Cider

6. Cactus

7. Seatown Seabar & Rotisserie

8. Hattie's Hat

9. Monsoon

10. RockCreek Seafood

How to Use This Book

ACH CHAPTER IN THIS book is dedicated to one area of the city, and each cocktail-slinging establishment within that area is listed alphabetically. Bar and restaurant reviews include the name, address, phone number, and website of the establishment. Bloody mary prices are listed as well as a review of their savory tomato cocktails, and if a restaurant has multiple locations, each location is listed at the end of the chapter in a section titled "Additional Locations."

Each review also contains a category icon and an answer to the question "Why go?" This allows you to quickly find the exact kind of bloody mary you crave.

Finally, as with many things in life, things change. Every effort has been made to verify the addresses, phone numbers, prices, and other information contained in this guide. However, before you begin your bloody mary filled journey, it is best to confirm the accuracy of this information.

It should go without saying, but be safe, drive safe, and drink safe.

CATEGORY KEY

BYO

BUILD YOUR OWN

MORE THAN ONE

AYCD

ALL YOU CAN DRINK

UNIQUE

BEER BACK

CHEAP

GARNISH

NORTH

FREMONT, GREEN LAKE, MAPLE LEAF, PHINNEY RIDGE, RAVENNA, UNIVERSITY DISTRICT & WALLINGFORD

9 MILLION IN UNMARKED BILLS

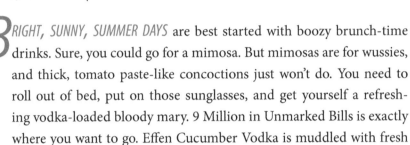

3507 Fremont Pl. N,. Seattle, WA 98103
(206) 632-0880 | 9m-unmarked.com

BRIGHT, SUNNY, SUMMER DAYS are best started with boozy brunch-time drinks. Sure, you could go for a mimosa. But mimosas are for wussies, and thick, tomato paste-like concoctions just won't do. You need to roll out of bed, put on those sunglasses, and get yourself a refreshing vodka-loaded bloody mary. 9 Million in Unmarked Bills is exactly where you want to go. Effen Cucumber Vodka is muddled with fresh basil leaves and juicy lime wedges to create a bright, summery drink to match the bright summer sun. One bite of the mild cherry pepper garnish, and you know you've started your day off right.

Why go? A refreshing cucumber bloody mary. | Price: $9

BLUE STAR CAFE & PUB

4512 Stone Way N., Seattle, WA 98103
(206) 548-0345 | bluestarcafeandpub.com

*W*ITH THREE DIFFERENT BLOODY marys to choose from, Blue Star Cafe lets you be as garnish crazy as you want to be. The "Traditional" is a simple, straight forward Demitri's bloody mary with no frills and just a hint of spice, the "Farmer's" includes a colorful bouquet of assorted pickled vegetables, and the "Chihuahua" kicks up its garnish game with pickled vegetables, cheese cubes, a big shrimp, and even a meat straw. As for why it's called the Chihuahua, I can only guess that the massive size of this bloody mary begins to approach the height of a small, yapping dog.

Why go? Garnish fun.
Price: Traditional $6, Farmer's $7.50, Chihuahua $10

BURGUNDIAN

2253 N. 56th St., Seattle, WA 98103
(206) 420-8943 | burgundianbar.com

MR. & MRS. T'S gets a bad rap, but I remember a time when it was pretty much as good as it gets for bottled mixes. With its robust flavor and salty juice, it was the perfect airport buddy and hangover-curing companion. Today, many mixes are vastly better, but I will always have a salty sweet spot in my heart for that groundbreaking mix. The "Burgundian House Bloody Mary" reminds me, in a good way, of a gourmet Mr. & Mrs. T's. Keeping in all the good and throwing away all the pasty, processed bad, the light, smooth consistency and big, bold flavor make this bloody mary the perfect daytime drink to cure what ails you. The only choice you have to make is vodka, gin, or tequila.

Why go? Salty gourmet. | *Price: $9*

DUKE'S CHOWDER HOUSE

7850 Green Lake Dr. N., Seattle, WA 98103
(206) 522-4908 | www.dukeschowderhouse.com

*D*UKE'S FAMOUS BLOODY MARY is described as "New Amsterdam vodka infused with roasted garlic and onions, black peppercorns, bell peppers, lemons and limes, mixed with Demitri's All-Natural Bloody Mary Seasoning, garnished with two jumbo prawns." And if that doesn't convince you, it's also tagged as "Our best selling Duketail ever." If you haven't tried Demitri's yet, I may just need to come slap some bloody mary sense into you. Demitri's Bloody Mary Seasoning is a unique product that, when combined with your choice of vodka and your favorite tomato juice, produces a perfectly mixed, perfectly balanced bloody mary that you can replicate with ease.

Why go? A kicked up Demitri's bloody mary. | Price: $9.40

SPOTLIGHT SEATTLE: DEMITRI'S BLOODY MARY SEASONING

I asked Demitri Pallis, founder of Demitri's Gourmet Mixes, two very important bloody mary questions.

What makes your bloody mary mix great?

"Our fresh, zesty, unmatchable flavor combined with our foolproof seasoning method makes Demitri's Bloody Mary Seasoning not just great but the most award-winning Bloody Mary on the planet. Our mixes are a gluten-free, kosher and contain 100% natural seasonings, and absolutely NO high fructose corn syrup, sulfites, MSG or anything artificial and unpronounceable."

What's your secret ingredient?

"Demitri's Bloody Mary Seasoning *is* the secret ingredient. Fourteen all-natural ingredients are masterfully balanced to create a perfect Bloody Mary. No more worrying about inconsistent flavor or quality, because we've done the hard part for you. Just add a shot of liquor, a splash of tomato juice, and you've got the perfect Bloody Mary every time, in no time."

EUREKA!

2614 NE 46th St., Seattle, WA 98105
(206) 812-9655 | www.eurekarestaurantgroup.com

*I*F YOU HAVE A cold or allergies or any other nasal congestion problem, I'd suggest you skip that trip to the Walgreens and instead, head over to Eureka! Their bloody mary is not just spicy, it's an intense, sinus-clearing session of horseradish assault on the senses. And it's cheaper than a pack of Dayquil. After your burning joy subsides, don't forget to admire the smiling face garnish letting you know, you made the right choice.

Why go? Horseradish assault.
Price: $5 on weekends, $10 on weekdays

FRANK'S OYSTER HOUSE & CHAMPAGNE PARLOR

2616 NE 55th St., Seattle, WA 98105
(206) 525-0220 | www.franksoysterhouse.com

*D*ESCRIBED SIMPLY AS "*VODKA,* classic ingredients," you know exactly what you'll be getting at Frank's Oyster House. A healthy pour of vodka blends seamlessly with a classic tomato mix to create a spicy bloody mary that relies on quality ingredients instead of garnish hype. Order up a side of oysters with bloody mary granita to create the perfect brunch time combo.

Why go? A classic bloody mary. | *Price: $9*

IVAR'S SALMON HOUSE

401 NE Northlake Way, Seattle, WA 98105
(206) 632-0767 | www.ivars.com

*H*ERE ARE THE DIRECTIONS, straight from Ivar's Salmon House. "Step 1: Order up your favorite vodka, tequila or gin. Step 2: Start from scratch with tomato juice or J. Wilbur Bloody Mary Mix. Step 3: Spice it up with a selection of over a dozen hot sauces, wasabi or horseradish. Step 4: Garnish away with Hickory smoked bacon, jumbo prawns, pepperoni, pickled asparagus, spicy green beans, blue cheese stuffed olives, pepperoncinis, celery, onions, citrus or whatever else you can throw at it." In my case, that "whatever else" just happened to be an eggs benedict pulled off the buffet line.

Why go? A build-your-own bloody mary. | Price: $8.50 and up

JOULE

3506 Stone Way N., Seattle, WA 98103
(206) 632-5685 | joulerestaurant.com

*D*EEP UMAME BASE SOUNDS like a Japanese techno band, but it's actually just the defining characteristic of Joule's bloody marys. A complex assortment of flavors are all perfectly blended so that not one ingredient stands out. It's the kind of bloody mary that you just can't quite put your finger on. If I had to guess, I'd say there was some sort of seaweed infusion, but I'd rather just leave you to hypothesize over your house beef jerky garnish.

Why go? Deep umame flavor. | *Price: $9*

THE MAPLE BAR

AYCD

8929 Roosevelt Way NE, Seattle, WA 98115
(206) 402-6135 | yelp.com/biz/the-maple-bar-seattle-3

*T*HE MAPLE BAR SPECIFICALLY caters to all the boozy day drinkers out there in Seattle land. On Saturdays and Sundays till 2PM, you'll get bottomless mimosas and bloody marys for just $14, and folks, this is one out of only two all-you-can-drink boozy brunch spots in the city. Sometimes, that means you're getting crappy drinks for a long period of time, but at Maple Bar, the quality of bloody mary stands tall, true and vodka-filled. With its chunky mix of horseradish, black pepper and cumin seed, Maple Bar's bloody mary provides full on flavor at a damn fine price.

Why go? AYCD bloody marys.
Price: $14 on weekends till 2:00 pm

NORM'S EATERY & ALE HOUSE

460 N. 36th St., Seattle, WA 98103
(206) 547-1417 | normseatery.com

I'M JUST GOING TO come right out with it. On weekends from 10AM - 2PM, this bloody mary is just four freakin' dollars. That's not just cheap. That's the cheapest possible price you will find for a half-way decent bloody mary. Super savory, salty, and hella spicy, this morning cocktail is exactly what you'd expect from a local, neighborhood bar. At this price point, I wouldn't expect much garnish, but Norm's still goes all out with a small array of crunchy pickled veg.

Why go? Cheap bloody marys.
Price: regularly $7, $4 on Sat. and Sun. 10-2pm

REVEL

403 N. 36th St., Seattle, WA 98103
(206) 547-2040 | www.revelseattle.com

*O*NE WORD. *K*IMCHI. *S*ALTY, sweet, spicy Kimchi. With an initial sweetness followed by an intense chili pepper flavor, Revel's "Kimchi Bloody Mary" envelopes your entire mouth with a biting, lingering spice. Nosh the burn away with a sweet, pickled green bean garnish, and pair it with a bacon donut and pork belly ramen for the perfect Asian fusion brunch.

Why go? Kimchi. | Price $8.

ROCKCREEK SEAFOOD & SPIRITS

4300 Fremont Ave. N., Seattle, WA 98103
(206) 557-7532 | www.rockcreekseattle.com

ROCKCREEK NOT ONLY HAS killer, fresh brunch-time bites, it also has bloody marys that exude creativity and innovation. The "Big Sky Bloody" is served with dill and rosemary vodka, house mary mix, a pickled shishito pepper, and a house pickle, while the "Big Sky Caesar" comes with a satisfyingly salty house Caesar mix. But if you truly want to get your bloody mary win on, ugprade to the "Baller Bloody or Caesar," served with a big ass poached prawn and oyster on the half shell.

Why go? Brunch. | Price: $10

STUMBLING GOAT BISTRO

6722 Greenwood Ave. N., Seattle, WA 98103
(206) 784-3535 | www.stumblinggoatbistro.com

*L*OADS OF FRESH CRACKED black pepper plus big horseradish chunks give the "Stumbling Goat Mary" a gritty burst of bloody mary flavor. But it doesn't stop there. A lemon-horseradish infused vodka provides big, bright citrus zest and even more horsey heat. A hint of dill and just a bit of spice bring it all together, and a delicately displayed pickled veg garnish finishes off this potent bloody mary.

Why go? Lemon-horseradish infused vodka.
Price: $7 during happy hour

WAYWARD VEGAN CAFE

801 NE 65th St., Seattle, WA 98115
(206) 524-0204 | www.waywardvegancafe.com

*V*EGAN BLOODY MARYS ARE hard to find and even harder to get right. But Wayward Vegan Cafe gets it done with Dicül brand bloody mary mix. Featuring an organic, vegan, and gluten-free blend, this mix combines fresh heirloom tomatoes, New Mexico's Hatch chili peppers, habanero, and more. It's basically a spicy, chunky, farmer's market basket of delectable summer veg. And here's the kicker. The special, secret ingredient is, wait for it, orange juice. Just let that one sink in.

Why go? A delicious vegan mix. | Price: $8

BALLARD

BALLARD ANNEX OYSTER HOUSE

5410 Ballard Ave. NW, Seattle, WA 98107
(206) 783-5410 | ballardannex.com

*O*YSTERS AND BLOODY MARYS go together like vodka and my liver. They mingle, they play, they complement each other in all the right ways. And Ballard Annex Oyster House knows just how to serve both with class and precision. Choose from (1) a bloody mary with Old Bay, a pickle, a thick slice of bacon, and Belvedere vodka or (2) a Bloody Caesar with Clamato, prawn garnish, celery, and Belvedere. Both are balanced with great viscosity and a quick spice, and both are exactly what you hope for from an oyster house bloody mary.

Why go? Oysters and Bloody Marys. | Price: $10

BASTILLE CAFE & BAR

5307 Ballard Ave. NW, Seattle, WA 98107

(206) 453-5014 | bastilleseattle.com

*F*OR SOME REASON, *I* walked into Bastille expecting a really terrible, poorly made, unimpressive bloody mary. So I was pleasantly surprised when an ultra-fresh, acidic tomato juice jolted my taste buds into action. Cracked black pepper and a zangy hit of lemon beat me with the flavor of a thousand brunches, while a quiet, sneaky heat eradicated any lingering doubt. In fact, all of my unfounded skepticism was promptly replaced with pure, unadulterated day-drinking joy.

Why go? Simple citrus joy. | *Price: $10*

BITTERROOT BBQ

5239 Ballard Ave. NW, Seattle, WA 98107

(206) 588-1577 | www.bitterrootbbq.com

*T*ASTING MORE LIKE A sorded affair of ketchup and cheap steak sauce, a bad BBQ bloody mary is just plain bad. But Bitterroot BBQ manages to pull off the incredible act of balancing sweet, smoky, savory, and spicy in their perfectly assembled Bitterroot Bloody Mary. Described as smoked tomato, house spices, pickled vegetables, and bacon jerky, this savory cocktail exemplifies exactly how smoky BBQ bloody marys should be served. A meaty garnish plus a smooth viscosity create the ultimate brunch time cocktail.

Why go? A BBQ mary done right. | Price: $10

EETBAR

1556 NW 56th St., Seattle, WA 98107

(206) 783-0131 | eetbar.com

*A*T EETBAR, CHOICE REIGNS supreme. Want house-made jalapeno vodka in your bloody mary? No problem. Want house-made garlic vodka? Sure! Want a mix of both? Sounds even better! Just start off with Clamato or Demitri's Bloody Mary Seasoning, and then begin assembling your dream tower of epic garnish. A variety of fresh and pickled veg, meats, cheeses, and even a beer chaser are all there for the taken. But if you really want to go all out, order EVERYTHING on the menu for just $12 more. You won't be needing that bacon and eggs platter.

Why go? A build-your-own bloody mary. | Price: $6 and up

HATTIE'S HAT

5231 Ballard Ave. NW, Seattle, WA 98107
(206) 784-0175 | hatties-hat.com

*S*UPER SAVORY WITH A deep rich flavor, Hattie's Hat gives you exactly what your aching hangover needs. And with a whopping seven different kinds, you'll have no problem finding a cocktail to suit all your bloody mary needs. Choose from (1) "Elsie's Famous Bloody Mary," (2) the "Rosemary Mary" with house-infused rosemary vodka, (3) the "2 Horses Mary" with house-infused horseradish vodka, (4) the "Ballard Mary" with Chang's Mighty Aquavit, (5) the "Five Alarm Mary" with house-infused Serrano Chile vodka, (6) the smoky "Mezcal Maria" with Ballard's Bonache Habanero Sauce, and (7) the Smoked Salmon Mary with Alaska Distillery's Smoked Salmon Vodka.

Why go? Bloody mary choices galore. | *Price: $8*

THE HI-LIFE

5425 Russell Ave. NW, Seattle, WA 98107
(206) 784-7272 | www.chowfoods.com/hi-life

*A*TTENTION BLOODY MARY ENTHUSIASTS, good luck finding a celery stalk in Seattle. Out of the 100+ bloody marys I drank in research for this book, a rough look at my notes shows that less than ten bloody marys were served with a fresh celery stalk. Thankfully, The Hi-Life knows that a good bloody mary deserves a fresh, crunchy celery stalk garnish. Featuring a "Firehouse Mary" with house-infused pepper vodka and a second seasonal bloody mary, such as the Summer Cucumber Mary, these bloody marys are savory, balanced, and always properly garnished.

Why go? CELERY!
Price: Firehouse Bloody Mary $8, seasonal bloody mary $8.50

KICKIN' BOOT WHISKEY KITCHEN

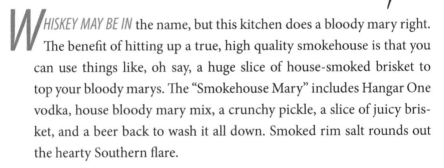

5309 22nd Ave. NW, Seattle, WA 98107
(206) 783-2668 | kickinboot.com

*W*HISKEY MAY BE IN the name, but this kitchen does a bloody mary right. The benefit of hitting up a true, high quality smokehouse is that you can use things like, oh say, a huge slice of house-smoked brisket to top your bloody marys. The "Smokehouse Mary" includes Hangar One vodka, house bloody mary mix, a crunchy pickle, a slice of juicy brisket, and a beer back to wash it all down. Smoked rim salt rounds out the hearty Southern flare.

Why go? Brisket. | Price: $8

KING'S HARDWARE

5225 Ballard Ave. NW, Seattle, WA 98107
(206) 782-0027 | www.kingsballard.com

KING'S HARDWARE IS THE kind of place you want to go after a near death experience. They'll pick you up, put a damn fine burger in your hand, and restore your will to live one 25 cent Skeeball game at a time. And on Sundays, they'll even serve you $4 bloody marys all day long. With its pickled green bean, carrot stick, olive, celery stalk, lemon and lime wedge, King's Hardware bloody marys are fully garnished with all the veg a bloody mary enthusiast could ask for. The mix itself is smooth and balanced with a medium spice and a fragrant celery salt aroma, making it easy to drink and easy to order two of.

Why go? A cheap, restorative bloody mary. | Price: $4 on Sundays

THE LEARY TRAVELER

4354 Leary Way NW, Seattle, WA 98107
(206) 783-4805 | www.learytraveler.com

*W*ITH TWO BLOODY MARYS to choose from, The Leary Traveler offers up both a mild mix for the cool at heart and a burning cocktail for those in need of a little spice. The "Veggie Supreme" is light but thirst-quench-ing, allowing the cooling Effen Cucumber vodka to shine through. Combined with a salty, dill-speckled mix, this bloody mary is perfect for joyous times. On the other hand, drinking the "Spicy Mamacita" is like inviting a cayenne-coated blow torch into the deepest recesses of your mouth, but I mean this in the best way possible.

Why go? Mild and spice, side by side. | Price: $9

PERCY'S & CO.

5233 Ballard Ave. NW, Seattle, WA 98107
(206) 420-3750 | www.percysseattle.com

WITH THEIR SUPER FRESH tomato mix and spicy full-bodied flavor, the bloody marys at Percy's attack your tongue with flavor swords of optimal satisfaction. Choose from (1) "Percy's Mary" with oregano-infused vodka, (2) the "Mother Mary" with dill-infused vodka, Dave's Hot Sauce, and brain tincture, (3) the "Spicy Maria" with cilantro-infused tequila, Dave's Hot Sauce, and complexion tincture and (4) the "Red Snapper" with thyme-infused gin, Dave's Hot Sauce, and energy tincture. Each bloody mary also includes house-made bloody mary mix along with fresh and pickled vegetables to match the cocktail's exact herbal infusion.

Why go? A fresh selection of herbaceous bloody marys. | *Price: $9*

PORKCHOP & CO.

5451 Leary Ave. NW, Seattle, WA 98107
(206) 257-5761 | www.eatatporkchop.com

KINDA HATE WHEN PLACES offer a small sized bloody mary, because well, who the hell wants a small amount of morning booze? I say, just go big or go home sober. Unfortunately, Porkchop & Co. does offer a small version of their super fresh "(Very) Spicy Bloody Mary," but I'll let it go, because they make up for it in all the right ways. As the name would suggest, this bloody mary is very spicy while still maintaining balance without overwhelming. A little bit of horseradish and a good vinegar-like hot sauce add a rich depth of flavor, and a bright tomato juice brings all that mouth-burning love straight to your eager, vodka-yearning belly.

Why go? Super fresh heat. | Price: small $6, large $9

RAY'S CAFE

6049 Seaview Ave. NW, Seattle, WA 98107
(206) 782-0094 | www.rays.com/cafe

*S*ERVING UP *"RAY'S BLOODY* Mary" with house-infused garlic vodka and classic Demitri's spicy bloody mary mix, Ray's Cafe gives you the perfect amount of savory and salty. Overlooking the Puget Sound, Ray's Cafe takes advantage of their succulent seafood abundance and perfectly pairs their bloody mary with a huge chunk of house-smoked salmon. The garlic is smooth and just barely detectable, and a light, thin tomato juice carries Demitri's seasoning throughout.

Why go? Demitri's with a twist.
Price: $9, add house-smoked salmon for $2

SKILLET DINER

2034 NW 56th St., Seattle, WA 98107
(206) 922-7981 | skilletstreetfood.com

*A*LL I HAVE TO say is: Bacon. Jam. Infused. Vodka. I could really stop there, but since we're chatting bloody marys, I'll elaborate. The light consistency and slightly smoky flavor make this bloody mary sultry, savory, and melded throughout. In other words, the bacon doesn't slap you in the face with a 700 lb hog. Rather, it lingers around each expanse of your salivating mouth, delivering juicy, luscious heat. A final touch of bacon salt rimmer make this bloody mary a delicious cocktail of bacon perfection.

Why go? Bacon times two. | Price: $10

VOLTERRA

5411 Ballard Ave. NW, Seattle, WA 98107
(206) 789-5100 | volterrarestaurant.com

*I*F YOUR OLD *I*TALIAN grandmother happened to be a bloody mary connoisseur, she'd no doubt be traveling to Volterra for a brunch-time cocktail like no other in Seattle. The "Bellisimo Bloody Mary" features tomato-garlic infused vodka, house-made balsamic bloody mary mix, fresh rosemary, and garlic stuffed olives for just $6. From the scent of herbaceous rosemary to the smooth tomato puree, each delectably sweet sip reminds you of the ultimate in Italian freshness.

Why go? An Italian style bloody mary. | Price: $6

ZAYDA BUDDY'S

5405 Leary Ave. NW, Seattle, WA 98107
(206) 783-7777 | zaydabuddyspizza.com

*Z*AYDA BUDDY'S CALLS ITS savory tomato cocktail "The Best Damn Bloody Mary," and it's damn good they lived up to the claim. A spicy mix is served with a self-described "small meal" of pickled treats, a cheese curd, and a cold lager chaser. Pair it with a plate of jalapeno tot poppers, and let your inner Midwest spirit be completely satisfied.

Why go? Fresh and simple. | *Price: $10*

CENTRAL

MADISON PARK, QUEEN ANNE & SOUTH LAKE UNION

BRAVE HORSE TAVERN

310 Terry Ave. N., Seattle, WA 98109
(206) 971-0717 | bravehorsetavern.com

*A*T BRAVE HORSE TAVERN, you have two choices. (1) "Dave's Bloody Mary" features pickled veggies, a mini beer back, and a bright red salty mix with robust tomato flavor. (2) With its smoky concoction of sweet oak and savory tomato, the "Bloody Scotsman" features Bank Note 5 year scotch and house mary mix. All you need is a hand-made pretzel with peanut butter bacon dip to complete this breakfast of champions.

Why go? A scotch bloody mary. | Price: $10.50

CACTUS - MADISON PARK

4220 E. Madison St., Seattle, WA 98112
(206) 324-4140 | www.cactusrestaurants.com

*C*ACTUS IS A SLEEPER. I've never heard anyone talk about their bloody marys, but quite frankly, they serve up some of the best bloody marys and marias in the city. Fresh jalapeno chunks brighten and bring long-lasting heat. A little bit of lime adds freshness without overwhelming, and a thick chipotle salt rim provides a fragrant smoky scent. But the ingredient that makes this bloody mary truly stand out is cilantro. Mark my words, you're going to start seeing a lot more cilantro in bloody marys.

Why go? Cilantro. | Price: $8 (add $1 for Belvedere vodka)

CAFE FLORA

2901 E. Madison St., Seattle, WA 98112
(206) 325-9100 | www.cafeflora.com

*T*HE FIRST THOUGHT YOU'LL have when sipping a Cafe Flora bloody mary is a cross between Keanu Reaves' "Whoa." and "What the hell is this?" Hints of lemongrass give you an initial Asian flare, but it's much more complex than that. Cucumber-jalapeno vodka, dill, cracked black pepper, light spice, and hints of tomato sweetness all meld together in a Twister party of palate-dancing flavor. A fully loaded garnish production comes with an assortment of pickled veg, a real marinated olive, and a nice spiced rimmer.

Why go? Unique flavors. | Price: $10

MECCA CAFE

526 Queen Anne Ave. N., Seattle, WA 98109
(206) 285-9728 | mecca-cafe.com

*N*O, IT'S NOT HAND-CRAFTED from the finest heirloom tomatoes. And no, it's not freshly muddled with organic herbs and spices. In fact, it's really just bloody mary seasoning with some added citrus. But damnit, Mecca's bloody mary is the perfect hangover-relieving, savory restoration you can get for $6.75. And with breakfast served all day, you can drink away your Tuesday afternoon with hangover-healing bloody marys and a greasy #7 with Bacon.

Why go? Hangover relief. | *Price: $6.75*

PESO'S KITCHEN & LOUNGE

605 Queen Anne Ave. N., Seattle, WA 98109
(206) 283-9353 | pesoskitchenandlounge.com

*P*ESO'S IS HANDS DOWN the place to go for a mouth-scorching, spicy bloody marys. The "Classic Bloody Mary" contains hot sauce and horseradish, loaded with Pearl vodka, while the "El Diablo Bloody Mary" contains house-infused seven pepper vodka and a rich tomato base. Both are smooth with nicely balanced, intricate flavors. But the El Diablo will burn your pretty little organic wool socks off.

Why go? Fresh and simple. | Price: $10

TAYLOR SHELLFISH OYSTER BAR

124 Republican St., Seattle, WA 98109
(206) 501-4442 | tayloroysterbars.com

*B*LOODY MARYS ON HAPPY hour plus a heavy pour of vodka equals one very happy bloody mary enthusiast. At each of Taylor Shellfish Bar's three locations, you'll be served a perfectly balanced bloody mary that is heavy on horseradish, vodka, and spicy afternoon goodness. Order up a plate of happy hour oysters for a briny snack of complementary chow.

Why go? Happy Hour. | Price: Regularly $9, Happy Hour $6

TOULOUSE PETIT

601 Queen Anne Ave. N., Seattle, WA 98109
(206) 432-9069 | toulousepetit.com

*T*OULOUSE *P*ETIT MAY BE known for its extensive happy hour menu ranging from Fried Chicken Gumbo to Spicy Lamb Sliders to Crawfish 'Beignets,' but you'd do well to also pick up one of their Creole bloody marys. Made with Pearl vodka, creole salt, and celery bitters, this light and fresh tomato mix is perfectly complemented by a complex spice blend and long, lemon finish. Light on salt and spice, this bloody mary is easy to drink any day of the week.

Why go? A Creole bloody mary. | Price: $9 before 4pm

ADDITIONAL LOCATIONS

Duke's Chowder House - Lake Union
901 Fairview Ave. N., Seattle, WA 98102 | (206) 382-9963

Sport Restaurant
140 4th Ave. N. #130, Seattle, WA 98109 | (206) 404-7767

CAPITOL HILL

BARRIO MEXICAN KITCHEN & BAR

1420 12th Ave., Seattle, WA 98122
(206) 588-8105 | www.barriorestaurant.com

*H*EAD TO *B*ARRIO, ORDER the Breakfast Chilaquiles, and prepare your insides for a slap of ghost chili reality as you consume this fiery pit of spicy maria love. Heavy spice is balanced with a slight sweetness and a very savory finish. Topped with jalapeno-stuffed olives, you're sure to warm up on even the dreariest of Seattle days.

Why go? Ghost chili tequila.
Price: Bloody Mary or Maria $9, Spicy Maria $10

BIMBO'S CANTINA

1013 E. Pike St., Seattle, WA 98122
(206) 322-9950 | www.bimboscantina.com

*N*OT ONLY DOES *BIMBO'S* Cantina have an impressively long margarita list, it also has an awesome all day happy hour on Sundays and Mondays featuring $5 bloody marys and marias. Slightly bitter and all savory, their mix features copious amounts of black pepper and a heavy celery salt presence. It is precisely the kind of bloody mary you want after a long night of copious imbibing. Just don't forget to ease that belly ache with a mini cheese quesadilla and side of "Stoner Nachos."

Why go? Cheap and savory. | *Price: $5 during Happy Hour*

CANTERBURY ALE HOUSE

534 15th Ave. E., Seattle, WA 98112
(206) 325-3110 | thecanterburyalehouse.com

AYCD

*W*ITH UNLIMITED BLOODY MARYS and mimosas till 2pm, Canterbury Ale House is exactly where you need to be spending your Sunday fun day. Very spicy with a hefty base, this bloody mary carries the spicy red liquid of drunken love straight through your mouth and into the depths of your vodka-craving soul. A little horseradish and lots of black pepper pieces accentuate the spice and a nice chunky salt rim provides the finishing touch. ,

Why go? Unlimited bloody marys.
Price: $8 each or $15 for AYCD on weekends till 2PM

CAPITOL CIDER

818 E. Pike St., Seattle, WA 98122
(206) 397-3564 | www.capitolcider.com

*C*HOICE #1: GET THE $10 Bloody Mary with Oola Rosemary Vodka, pickled carrot, and celery. Choice #2: Get the $12 Bloody Mary Flight with Tequila, Mezcal, and Gin. Choice #3: Go Drunken Tomato style, and convince your brunch buddies to split all four! For a smooth, balanced and classic bloody mary, Capitol Cider's "Rosemary Bloody Mary" will fulfill all your boozy brunch needs. But if a more adventurous experience is what you're after, order up the bloody mary flight. The gin provides complexity and herbaceousness, the tequila, well, tastes like tequila, and bloody mary mix, and the mezcal provides a strong, smoky smell.

Why go? Vodka, gin, tequila, and mezcal.
Price: Bloody Mary $10; Bloody Mary Flight $12

COASTAL KITCHEN

429 15th Ave. E., Seattle, WA 98112
(206) 322-1145 | coastalkitchenseattle.com

GENERALLY TRY TO RESERVE my tequila intake for beach-side margaritas, but Coastal Kitchen changes all that with its Caribbean Maria. Featuring house-infused pepper cilantro tequila, spiced tomato, fresh cilantro and peppers, and a heavy dose of lime juice, this breakfast bloody mary is the tequila sunrise of brunch time drinks. Even better, if you stop by from 8-10AM, Monday through Friday, you'll get happy hour breakfast cocktails for just $5!

Why go? House-infused pepper cilantro tequila.
Price: Spicy bloody mary $8, Caribbean Maria $10

GRIM'S PROVISIONS & SPIRITS

1512 11th Ave., Seattle, WA 98122
(206) 324-7467 | www.grimseattle.com

GRIM'S DOESN'T SKIMP WHEN it comes to big, pickled garnish. Lemon, lime, pickled green beans, olives, a pepperoncini, and a full pickle top this mason jar bloody mary. Strong and very spicy, the lingering heat and flowing tomato juice make this bloody mary perfectly suited for long bouts of day-drinking fun.

Why go? A garnish bonanza. | *Price: $8*

LINDA'S TAVERN

707 E. Pine St., Seattle, WA 98122
(206) 325-1220 | www.lindastavern.com

*L*INDA'S *T*AVERN PUMPS OUT a salty, savory, hangover ass-kicking mix of epic salt proportions. Black pepper bits and a hint of horseradish wake up your dulled senses from a night of cheerful excess. A lingering, burning heat makes sure you know it's time to start drinking again. And for a dollar more, you can upgrade to the Bufflao Mary, topped with a big piece of buffalo jerky to give you all the energy you need to keep the party going.

Why go? Savory, salty hangover relief.
Price: $8, add $1 for Buffalo Mary

LOST LAKE CAFE & LOUNGE

1505 10th Ave., Seattle, WA 98122
(206) 323-5678 | lostlakecafe.com

24 HOUR DINERS HOLD a very special place in my heart. Lost Lake Cafe is the kind of place where you can still get early bird specials like a Cheeseburger and Fries for $2.99, a breakfast sandwich for just $3.25, and a pint-sized bloody mary for a solid five bucks. But if you don't happen to wake up that early, just upgrade to the "Lost Lake Mary" with Capitol Hill's Oola Pepper vodka, house pickled veggies, and a celery salted rim. The pepper vodka may seem a bit strange at first but trust me, it grows on you.

Why go? Breakfast Happy Hour.
Price: regularly $8, $5 from 6 - 9am M- F; add $2 for Lost Lake

MANHATTAN

1419 12th Ave., Seattle, WA 98122

(206) 325-6574 | www.manhattanseattle.com

*A*T MANHATTAN, YOUR BIGGEST problem will be deciding which of the five different bloody marys you should choose. Your options include: (1) the "Manhattan Bloody Mary" with vodka, bacon, and a sriracha-dotted prawn, (2) the "Kentucky Mary" with bourbon, BBQ sauce, and bacon (3) the "Red Snapper" with Gin, (4) the "Bloody Fairy" with absinthe, and (5) the "Bloody Beer" with draft lager. Each bloody mary also includes the savory house creole bloody mary mix, a bright red rimmer, and pickled veggie garnish.

Why go? Variety. | *Price: $7-15*

MONSOON

615 19th Ave. E., Seattle, WA 98112

(206) 325-2111 | www.monsoonrestaurants.com

*D*EEMED THE "BLOODY ALTERNATIVE," Monsoon's bloody mary is like no other. Featuring gin, kummel, pho broth, and sangrita, this is by far the most innovative bloody mary in all of Seattle. Gin adds a hint of herbal flare, while kummel adds sweetness with hints of caraway, cumin, and fennel. Pho broth brings it all together in an herbal medley of savory delight.

Why go? Pho. Price $10

SAINT JOHN'S BAR AND EATERY

719 E. Pike St., Seattle, WA 98122
(206) 245-1390 | www.saintjohnsseattle.com

S AINT JOHN'S OFFERS A house bloody mary with your choice of spirit. Go with the "Mary" for a traditional vodka take, the "Maggie" for London Gin, the "Maria" with Lunazul Tequila, or the "Mare" with horseradish-infused vodka. But just a word of warning, the horseradish vodka is intense. Like, "I'm glad I really like horseradish" intense, or "should I really be drinking this?" intense, or perhaps, more practically, "I guess I won't be needing that Sudafed any time soon" intense.

Why go? Horseradish assault. | *Price: $7*

SPOTLIGHT SEATTLE: SEATTLE PICKLE CO.

I asked Chris Coburn, owner of Seattle Pickle Co., two very important bloody mary questions.

What makes your bloody mary mix great?

"If you have tried other store bought mixes, you would find that they are very sweet, very salty or very sweet and salty. This is because many of those mixes were developed based on Southern US tastes. At Seattle Pickle Co., we really wanted to create a bloody mary mix that represented the Pacific Northwest Region. With its peppery hot kick, pickle brine and fresh whole seasonings, Smitty's Mary Mix captures the "Combined & Brined" sweet-briny saltiness of the Pacific Ocean in the Puget Sound and the fertile land that supports the many farms in the region."

What's your secret ingredient?

"Our secret is the combination of two main ingredients: Smitty herself, a local Seattleite, who crafted her bloody mary mix recipe through her experience as a fourth generation pickler, and our pickle brine. Don't underestimate the power of the pickle. Mix three parts bloody mary mix, with one part vodka and garnish with a Seattle Pickle Co. pickle for the perfect craft cocktail."

SAM'S TAVERN

1024 E. Pike. St., Seattle, WA 98122
(206) 397-3344 | samstavernseattle.com

CONSISTENTLY VOTED AS ONE of the best bloody marys in Seattle, Sam's Tavern is a must-visit for any dedicated bloody mary enthusiast. Sam's "Bakon Bloody Masterpiece" is topped with a slider, olive, onion, tomato, cheese cube, cocktail weenie, celery stalk, and lime wedge. But the garnish is just the beginning. The smoky Bakon vodka adds rich, meaty heft, and a moderate heat mixes well with the robust tomato blend. Just make sure you show up hungry.

Why go? An epic empire of garnish. | *Price: $14*

SUN LIQUOR DISTILLERY

512 E. Pike St., Seattle, WA 98122
(206) 720-1600 | sunliquor.com

*Y*OU'VE GOT TWO OPTIONS when brunching at Sun Liquor Distillery. One is the regular ol' bloody mary, and the other is made with Sun Liquor's in-house UNXLD vodka. You're at Sun Liquor, so you might as well get the good stuff. A deep savory flavor is met by a briny, bright acidity and a spicy finish. House-made pickled garnish is exceptionally crunchy and includes a delicious curried carrot and cauliflower, while a thick salt rim brings it all together with perfect execution.

Why go? Damn fine vodka with a curry garnish. | *Price: $11*

TERRA PLATA

1501 Melrose Ave., Seattle, WA 98122
(206) 325-1501 | terraplata.com

I HAVE A SPECIAL PLACE in my heart for Gordon's vodka. In fact, my puggle puppy is even named after it. Terra Plata uses that very same vodka but thankfully, they add many more pleasing ingredients to it. The spicy bloody mary comes with a heavy helping of sriracha, a big cheese cube, and a hunk of whatever charcuterie is on hand, while the regular is a cumin-soaked powerhouse with hints of sweetness, smokiness, and black pepper chunks. Both are topped with a nice selection of pickled veggies, and both give you something you're not quite expecting.

Why go? A unique bloody mary. | Price: regular $9, spicy $11

TALLULAH'S

550 19th Ave. E., Seattle, WA 98112
(206) 860-0077 | www.aneighborhoodcafe.com

*L*IGHT TOMATO FLAVOR COMBINES with a bright tobasco-like heat to deliver a simple but savory bloody mary. Vinegar kicks your sleepy taste buds into gear while a moderate spice, with just a touch of salt, adds overall flavor. Simplicity is the winner here with a straight forward garnish of olive, lemon, lime, and a bright red salted rim.

Why go? Simplicity with an edge. | *Price: $8*

ADDITIONAL LOCATIONS

Skillet - Capitol Hill
1400 E. Union St., Seattle, WA 98122 | (206) 512-2001

Taylor Shellfish Oyster Bar - Capitol Hill
1521 Melrose Ave., Seattle, WA 98101 | (206) 501-4321

DOWNTOWN

BELLTOWN, DOWNTOWN, PIKE PLACE MARKET & PIONEER SQUARE

THE 5 POINT CAFE

415 Cedar St., Seattle, WA 98121
(206) 448-9991 | the5pointcafe.com

*5*POINT'S BLOODY MARY IS not for the weak of heart or the weak of stom-
ach. Salty J. Wilbur bloody mary seasoning is mixed with more salt,
pepper, and hit of Secret Aardvark Habanero Hot Sauce to create a super savory, super salty cocktail that is fit to fix all your hangover woes.
Hit up breakfast happy hour from 6-9AM Monday through Friday for
discounted $5 bloody marys. But if your morning starts at 2PM, don't
worry. 5 Point bloody marys are always just $8.

Why go? A salty mix. | Price: regularly $8, happy hour $5

BELL + WHETE

200 Bell St., Seattle, WA 98121
(206) 538-0180 | www.bellandwhete.com

*F*IND YOURSELF A GROUP of six dedicated bloody mary enthusiasts, and get your determined selves to Bell + Whete for no less than six different kinds of bloody marys. Choose from (1) the "Archbishop" with house-made pickles and landjager, (2) the "Foreman" with smoked tomato, bacon, onion, and porter, (3) the "Drake" with tomatillo, fennel, celery, and garlic, (4) the "Garth" with carrot, radish, orange, curry spice, and cider, (5) the "Ivar" with tomato, clam juice, lime, dill, and lager and (6) the Ottoman with roasted red pepper, tomato, kale, and harissa spice.

Why go? Six unique bloody marys. | Price: $8

DELICATUS

103 1st Avenue South, Seattle, WA 98104
(206) 623-3780 | www.delicatusseattle.com

*D*ELICATUS DOES A BLOODY mary like no other bloody mary in Seattle. In-house pepper infused vodka is matched with a robust tomato base, lots of freshly cracked black pepper, and a fragrant cumin rimmer. But to add even more richness to this deeply savory drink, Delicatus adds one very unique ingredient: lamb stock. Bringing a rich, meaty flavor of heft and spice, the lamb stock not only enhances this already savory cocktail, it makes it truly one of a kind.

Why go? Lamb stock . | Price: $8

ETTA'S

2020 Western Ave., Seattle, WA 98121

(206) 443-6000 | tomdouglas.com/restaurants/ettas

*E*TTA'S SERVES UP *(1)* "Etta's Bloody Mary" with house Prosser Farm pepper-infused vodka and fresh horseradish and (2) the "Pike Place Mary" with house mary mix, Bavarian meats land jaeger, smoked Beecher's jack, and a Pike Place Pale Ale beer back. There's definitely more overall spice in the Pike Place. Both are light, fresh, and easy to drink, but the added beer back and meat and cheese garnish make the Pike Place Mary the clear winner.

Why go? Light and fresh with a beer back.
Price: Etta's Bloody Mary $10.50, Pike Place $12.50

LOLA

2000 4th Ave., Seattle, WA 98121
(206) 441-1430 | tomdouglas.com/restaurants/lola

*B*ALANCE IS DIFFICULT TO achieve. Whether you're talking about career/family, work/life, time vs. pretty much anything else, or getting a bloody mary just right, care and precision must always be taken. Seamlessly put together, Lola manages to achieve the purple unicorn of classic bloody marys. Light but rich with a good long heat and celery salt rim, Lola's bloody mary makes the perfect accompaniment to both savory and sweet brunch-time bites.

Why go? Balance. | *Price $10.50*

LOWELL'S RESTAURANT

Pike Place Market, 1519 Pike Pl., Seattle, WA 98101
(206) 622-2036 | eatatlowells.com

*L*OWELL'S SERVES UP NO less than five unique, scratch-made bloody marys including (1) the "Lowell's Classic" with premium triple-distilled vodka, (2) the "Hangtown Mary" with bacon-infused vodka and a fresh Pacific Northwest oyster, (3) the "Chili Mary" with spicy serrano chili-infused vodka, (4) the "Rosemary Fennel Mary" with fresh fennel and rosemary infused vodka, and (5) the "Smoked Salmon Mary" with fresh, wild Alaskan King salmon infused vodka. Show up early for a seat overlooking the Puget Sound, and get you bloody mary drink on.

Why go? A smoked salmon bloody mary. | Price: $8-10

MATT'S IN THE MARKET

Pike Place Market, 94 Pike St. #32, Seattle, WA 98101
(206) 467-7909 | www.mattsinthemarket.com

*M*ATT'S IN THE MARKET not only offers great respite from the often chaotic Pike Place Market, it also offers a damn fine "Robbie's Bloody Mary with a Snit." For those that don't know what a snit is, you'll probably best understand it as a nip, snert or, more commonly, a beer back. Flavors of sweet, salty, savory, and acidity all interact with a complexity similar to locating the gum wall via Google Maps. A Mama Lil's pickled green bean tops it all off for that final crunchy finish.

Why go? Complexity with a snit. | Price: $10

PALOMINO

1420 5th Avenue, Seattle, WA 98101
(206) 623-1300 | www.palomino.com

*P*ALOMINO NOT ONLY HOSTS a very generous happy hour, it also puts together a high class bloody mary. The "Palomino Bloody Mary" includes Stoli hot jalapeno vodka, house-smoked pepperoni, Kalamata olives, and herb salt. But the clear star of this savory tomato show is the giant smoked mozz garnish. Soft and bouncy to the touch, it emanates charred, smoky flavor and pairs perfectly with the spicy vodka selection.

Why go? A hot and cheesy bloody mary. | Price: $9

SEATOWN SEABAR & ROTISSERIE

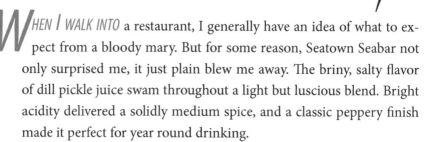

2010 Western Ave., Seattle, WA 98121
(206) 436-0390 | tomdouglas.com

*W*HEN *I* WALK INTO a restaurant, I generally have an idea of what to expect from a bloody mary. But for some reason, Seatown Seabar not only surprised me, it just plain blew me away. The briny, salty flavor of dill pickle juice swam throughout a light but luscious blend. Bright acidity delivered a solidly medium spice, and a classic peppery finish made it perfect for year round drinking.

Why go? Pickle juice. | Price: $10.50

TILIKUM PLACE CAFE

407 Cedar St., Seattle, WA 98121
(206) 282-4830 | www.tilikumplacecafe.com

*T*ILIKUM'S BLOODY MARY IS described as "house-made bloody mary mix, with our own spicy pepper medley infused vodka." But compared to some of Seattle's other mouth-scorching cocktails, you shouldn't really be thinking fiery raw serrano spicy, but rather a roasted jalapeno spicy. Howerver, even more than that, you should be thinking about the deliciously blackened cocktail onion that comes skewered upon your glass. So small, simple, and deeply flavorful, you may just have to pay $10 for the privilege of tasting it.

Why go? An exceptional cocktail onion. | Price: $10

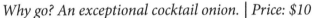

TWISTED PASTY

2525 4th Ave., Seattle, WA 98121
(206) 402-3831 | www.twistedpasty.com

*T*WISTED *P*ASTY FEATURES A weekend build-your-own bloody mary bar where you can practice your hand at building the ultimate garnish topped cocktail. But if you're not the best bloody mary builder just yet, you can still leave it up to the bartending professionals. Just make sure you ask for the house jalapeno-infused vodka for that extra kick of spice.

Why go? A build-your-own with spice. | *Price: $9*

WEST SEATTLE & SOUTH

COLUMBIA CITY, GEORGETOWN & WEST SEATTLE

THE BRIDGE

6301 California Ave. SW, Seattle, WA 98136
(206) 402-4606 | www.thebridgeseattle.com

*T*HE BRIDGE IS THAT kind of place where some guy will literally buy the whole bar a round of ridiculously large shots of terrible liquor on an early Saturday afternoon. In other words, it's my kind of bar. Friendly and sociable, the bartender will shake your hand and introduce himself by name before serving up one of three carefully assembled bloody marys. The "Classic Bloody" includes standard garnish additions, the "Garden Mary" comes with pickled veg galore, and the "Bacon Mary" is topped with a big slice of house-cured maple bacon.

Why go? Boozy bloody marys with friends.
Price: Classic Mary $7, Garden Mary $8, Bacon Mary $9

FRESH BISTRO

4725 42nd Ave. SW, Seattle, WA 98116
(206) 935-3733 | www.freshbistroseattle.com

*L*ET ME PUT IT this way. When I happened upon Fresh Bistro, it was as if the celery salt seas had parted, revealing a glowing crimson wellspring of drunken brunch joy. Described as "House Infused Thai Chili Vodka, House Made Bloody Mix, Kimchi Salted Rim, Sriracha Pickled Apple," this $8 bloody mary brings a serious complexity of flavors. Acidic but savory, light in texture but full-bodied in flavor, a moderate spice combo of both horseradish and chili pepper... basically every bloody mary descriptor I can think of is in here. And to top it all off, a unique sriracha-pickled apple and sweet pickled asparagus spear provide a healthy pre-brunch snack.

Why go? A fresh and fun bloody mary. | *Price: $8*

GEORGETOWN LIQUOR COMPANY

5501 Airport Way S., Seattle, WA 98108
(206) 763-6764 | georgetownliquorco.com

A T GEORGETOWN LIQUOR COMPANY, it's all about the tangy citrus flavor. Bloody mary staples, such as V-8 and freshly muddled lemon and lime wedges, are added to sweet, tangy A.1. Steak Sauce and spicy Secret Aardvark Habanero Hot Sauce. The result is a zesty combination of rich, savory flavor with a biting BBQ-like acidity. A huge pickled asparagus spear finishes off this pint-sized bloody mary.

Why go? A.1. | Price: $9

HUDSON

5000 E. Marginal Way S., Seattle, WA 98134

(206) 725-0519 | www.hudsonseattle.com

*W*HEN YOU'RE IN THE Midwest, there's only one way to serve a bloody mary: with a beer back. Hudson serves their bloody mary in true Midwest fashion with Burnett's vodka, fresh limes, real horseradish, a dash of hot sauce, celery salt, and, of course, a Miller High Life beer back. With lots of pepper, heaps of horseradish, and a few dashes of Crystal brand hot sauce, this bloody mary is sharply acidic and ready for some Midwestern love.

Why go? A Midwest style bloody mary. | *Price: $7.50*

LOTTIE'S LOUNGE

4900 Rainier Ave. S., Seattle, WA 98118
(206) 725-0519 | www.lottieslounge.com

*S*EVEN DIFFERENT BLOODY MARYS graze the menu of Lottie's Lounge, including the classic, wasabi, bloody maria, cucumber, hellfire, basil, and beet. You can't go wrong with any choice, but if you've never had the pleasure of imbibing a beet-flavored bloody mary, then you're missing out. Lending a slightly sweet, hearty, and earthy flavor, the beet vodka accentuates the robust tomato juice and creates a bright red, glowing cocktail.

Why go? Unique vodka infusions. | *Price: $8*

SHADOWLAND

4458 California Ave. SW, Seattle, WA 98116
(206) 420-3817 | mainstreethub.com/shadowlandwest

*D*EEP SAVORY FLAVOR MAKES Shadowland's bloody mary perfect for brooding winter days. Served in a tall pint glass with two olives and a lime wedge, you'll not only dodge any bouts of scurvy (yes, it's still a thing), you'll also get a mid-morning treat. Spicy and peppery with just a little horseradish, this bloody mary has enough heat to waken all your dulled senses and keep you going through the fifth, sixth, or even seventh day of your week-long bender.

Why go? Savory sustenance. | Price: $6

TALARICO'S PIZZERIA

4718 California Ave. SW, Seattle, WA 98116
(206) 937-3463 | talaricospizza.com

*E*NORMOUS PIZZA SLICES MEET giant bloody marys at this East Coast style pizzeria. Order your choice of four goblet-sized bloody marys including (1) "Talarico's House Bloody Mary" with J. Wilber's special blend of spices, (2) the "Spicy Italian Mary" with house-infused chili-pepper vodka and an Italian herbed Mary mix, (3) "The Bloody Caesar" with Clamato juice, and (4) "The Bloody Hog" with bacon-infused vodka and a slice of candied bacon. Each bloody mary also features J. Wilber's slightly sweet and slightly spicy seasoning and is garnished with two types of peppers and an olive.

Why go? Big, savory bloody marys. | *Price: $10*

WEST 5

4539 California Ave. SW, Seattle, WA 98116
(206) 935-1966 | yelp.com/biz/west-5-seattle

*W*EST 5 HAS, HANDS down, the absolutely best classically styled bloody mary that Seattle has to offer. Sure, it's Campbell's tomato juice and yeah, it's just the standard bloody mary ingredients. But this hearty classic hits all the right stops. A standard garnish of olives, pickled green beans, and a lime wedge suits the classic formulation.

Why go? The best classic bloody mary recipe in Seattle.
Price: $7.50

ADDITIONAL LOCATIONS

Cactus - Alki Beach
2820 Alki Ave SW, Seattle, WA 98116 | (206) 933-6000

Duke's Chowder House - Alki
2516 Alki Ave SW, Seattle, WA 98116 | (206) 937-6100

ACKNOWLEDGMENTS

*T*HANK YOU TO EACH and every one of my fellow bloody mary enthusiasts for accompanying me on this bloody mary filled journey. Thank you to Ryan Armstrong, for your sweet editing skills and ever-supportive chats. And finally, thank you to Gould for encouraging me to drink ALL the bloody marys.

ABOUT THE AUTHOR

*S*HELLEY BUCHANAN IS THE author of The Drunken Tomato book series and the founder of DrunkenTomato.com. She is a former Portlander, New Yorker and Los Angeleno currently residing in a tiny, over-priced Seattle apartment. She enjoys writing, short walks on the beach and well-garnished bloody marys. If you want to know more, you'll have to buy her a drink first.

CPSIA information can be obtained at www.ICGtesting.com
Printed in the USA
LVOW01s2306130915

454007LV00006B/11/P